I0088401

no apologies

ja carter-winward

Binary Press 2013

Published by Binary Press Publications, LLC

ISBN-13: 978-1-61171-021-2

ISBN-10: 1611710219

dedication

This work is dedicated to anyone and everyone

who has bumped, rubbed or crashed into me.

You helped me, in your own way, create a beautiful monster.

scars

i walked in
on his bachelor party in the back room
of the bar.
it was just him, his older brother
and his dad.
i did a striptease for them
because every bachelor party
ought to have a stripper,
but i left my
g-string on.
i took him home
and i told him he was too young
to get married to a woman
with a kid.
he believed me
so he didn't marry her.
after he ditched his wedding
he seemed sort of lost
so we hung out together.
his cock was small
and women who say size doesn't matter
are fucking lunatics.
but he tried
and i opened my legs for effort.
one morning
i looked at his chest
and he had scars by his nipples.
i asked him about them
and he wouldn't tell me what they were
but i think they had something to do
with his little cock
and why he wanted to get married
so fucking young.

amy

i was in love with this one girl
from grade school all the way
through high school.
i was obsessed
with her tits.
they were firm
and had big, swollen nipples
and they had this up-sweep
like they were turning their noses
up at me.
she did a lot of drugs
in college i think
because when we spoke again
in our 40's
she seemed just off, like
not all of the cylinders were pumping.
but i liked talking to her
and somehow i found a time to confess
to her how i'd felt about her growing up.
she was flattered
and even suggested we get together.
but she was in the east bay in california
and i was in utah
so it didn't seem likely.
i'm pretty sure there were a shit load of people
who had it pretty bad for her.
she killed herself
and left behind
a seven year old son.
she left behind
all of us
who had wanted her
and saw something in her
that made us yearn.

rice garden

hector is a tanned mole rat of a man
wearing his stained apron
outside
the chinese take-out joint.
he takes smoke breaks
out the side door
and every day he feels lucky
because there's a small cement wall
to lean on
and trees overhead
to fight the sun.
it's in a small alley
so there's not much traffic.
hector measures his days
in smoke breaks
and large take-out orders
from the law office
three doors down.
he takes his break
before they pick up
and he gets to watch
the brunette with tight pants
walk over from the office
and pick up the order.
he watches her and that measures another
small,
incremental part of the day.
when she comes
he knows he only has
four more hours
until he can go home.

two days

we drank
got high and did blow
we watched t.v. and ordered
pizza.
my kids were coming home
in two days
and i had to go to work.
i looked around
and saw all of this shit
and people
noise and nothing
and my body was foreign.
my body wasn't the body
of a mother.
i left
but i didn't know how i would clean up
my insides
because they felt
totally
polluted.
i didn't want my kids
smelling it
as it oozed out of my pores.

∽∾

tiny words

My children had an uncanny way
of saying things
like most kids-
lellow (yellow),
hangerber,
rhinocinos,
pahsketti,
pocacoocoo (pocahontas)-
i wanted to strangle the person
who finally corrected them.
but
i suppose
it was inevitable.

drunk

i was wasted at this party
and saw a guy who was my friend-
we'd hung out together a lot
and i really liked him
as a friend.
i grabbed him by the hand
and took him to a bedroom
and asked him to fuck me.
he said he couldn't
because we were friends
and i was drunk.
later on
he gave me this big long letter
about why he wouldn't fuck me that night.
it was pretty fucking mushy
and sweet
and sad
and i felt bad i couldn't
feel that way about him.
later on he told me
if he'd known that was his one chance
he would have done it.
i think we've all been there-
that one fucking chance
to say it
feel it
fuck it
do it.
and we miss it because
we don't know
that whatever's right in front of us
is all there is.

৩৫

show and tell

he was my jujitsu instructor
and so he spent a lot of time
between my legs anyway.
he'd been raised catholic
and catholic-sex-guilt
is way worse than
mormon-sex-guilt
so he was naïve for 43.
i wasn't very good at jujitsu
but he liked me anyway
so one day he drove me home
on his motorcycle
and in my apartment
we talked about fantasies.
he told me he'd never seen
a woman get herself off.
so i showed him.
i was really good at that.

❧

ruined

when rosie
fingered dawn
it ruined the literary
reference for me
completely.

quarters

it was a small apartment
and the smoke was so thick
it was a fog.
we played quarters
and no one knew
that i didn't want to be there.
didn't want to be home
either
because i choked
on a different fog there.
i got pretty fucked up
because i wasn't good at quarters
and i left.
i started walking down the sidewalk
past this brownstone church on 4th east
with my hands jammed in my pockets
and soon i started to run
but no matter how fast i went
i always caught up
to myself.

warning

her name was becky
and she was the teacher for me and
a group of other girls at church.
she was only 19 but she had already
been married a year.
she told us that she had
a close encounter with
satan.
she was dating her then-future husband
and he'd proposed
and when she got back to her dorm
she suddenly got really cold
in her bed.
her hand was hanging off of the mattress
and she felt a pressure around her wrist
while a heavy, dark force
seemed to push her down
making her breathless.
she said it was the devil
trying to keep her
from marrying this guy.
she prayed
and the dark feeling went away.
this story seriously fucked
with my mind after that.
i still can't hang my hand
off of the bed at night.
i don't know why
the devil was so interested in her
and whether or not she married that guy.
they had four kids
and later on down the road
he embezzled a shitload of money
from his company
and got sent to jail.
she divorced him
and it made me wonder
if the evil presence she felt
while she was dating him
wasn't just a bad feeling
that she was having
because she was about to marry
a fucking criminal.

tricks

we had a dog named lady
when i was growing up.
other than the early morning barking
joining the chorus of other neighborhood
dogs
she was a pretty good dog.
whenever she had to go outside
she'd scratch at our kitchen door
to be let out.
for some reason lady was really scared
of my dad.
he would bend at the waist and talk to her
in a sweet voice
and she would proceed to do
every trick in her repertoire for him
before running to the kitchen door.
right at 5 o'clock
when he'd be arriving home
she'd run to the kitchen door
scratch scratch.
my dad was hard to live with
and every one of us as teens
clashed
horribly with him
even though he was only doing what he thought
was right.
my dad loved so many of us
and still
we were always trying
to get away-
we all had our kitchen doors
to escape him.

ৡঌ

break-up

he asked to meet me for coffee.
on some level i knew
but i decided to make it my move
to break it off.
i gathered his books
his tapes
and his t-shirt
that still smelled like him
and i headed to 9th and 9th
to say goodbye.
we sat in the shop for only a moment
then took his car
and drove to a church to talk.
he was confused,
he said.
he needed to clean the slate.
there was another woman.
and me?
i was his uncomplicated weekend
fuck
who happened to be
in love with him.
i didn't want anything from him
anyway
but he had all of these loose ends,
he said.
needed to tidy up.
needed to date
what's-her-face
and see if she still
healed his heart
the way she had 10 years ago.
it's best to maintain one's dignity
in these cases
but i cried anyway.
and then, for good measure
we did a good-bye fuck in his car
because our sex wasn't like
anything either of us had had
before and it would have been a shame
not to leave it on that note.
back at the coffee shop
i tried to give him his stuff back.

he said he didn't want it
so there was no closing that
gaping wound for good.
i drove home and listened to
norah jones sing
i don't miss you at all
and tried to forget
that i had been on a slate
and had been cleaned off
like so much dust.

❧

drama

i told my older sister
how i was really fucked up
and i drove down the canyon
and didn't give a fuck if i went over
the edge
because i was so depressed.
i was so in love with the drama of it
i didn't see her response coming.
she said
i wouldn't have gone over the edge
i would have hit a car full of kids
with a mother driving
just like her
and that was the very end of my
drunk-driving days.

໑ຉ

the moose

the place to be
in wyoming
was teton village.
the mangy moose had great bands.
i was introduced to white russians
by that actor john corbett
as he felt me up
under the table.
i went up to the second level
bar
and the bartender told me
he'd make me a free drink
if i showed him my tits.
i lifted my shirt
because they're just tits
and i had my second white russian
ever.

incommunicado

a friend of mine
wrote me
and asked me for a loan.
it felt
like a slug in my gut.
i had given her money before
and so i searched for all
of the emails we've exchanged
over the past five years
and i was wrong-
i'd given her money three times.
i knew
because the only emails she sent
were about money.
i didn't write her back
because i had so many things to say-
things about betrayal
and feeling used
and feeling
taken advantage of
and we didn't have the history
of talking
about anything like that.

ত্ত্

dentist

it's a huge fucking leap
working on someone's teeth
and then sticking your hand
down their shirt.
he was willing to take it
because it was a saturday
and his assistant
wasn't there.

if i could talk
to my parents again

i would tell them
i have food
and they never have to worry about
that for me again.
i would tell them
i experience a lot more joy
and contentment
than i thought was possible.
i would tell them
they were thrown a massive
curve-ball with me
but that they did alright-
better than alright.
i'd tell them about my family,
about my work.
i'd say i'm so, so sorry
for ages 12-30.
i'd tell them
that talking to them
was the most comforting
thing in the world.
i'd say thank you
for loving me when i was
unlovable.
i'd tell them
i'm finally listening to what they
tried to teach me
and that i'm teaching my kids
the same things.
i'd tell them
that now that they're gone
i am in awe of them
and all they sacrificed for me.
then i think i'd tell them
that they can rest, now.
they did it.
and we're all
going to be okay
because they showed up
when it mattered most.

life

i chose living a life
of significance
rather
than a life of happiness.
what is happiness
anyway
but having your mind
on something
that distracts you
from your purpose?

∽❧

monogamy

over a glass of red wine
he told me
he could never be monogamous.
it scared the living shit
out of me and made me realize
i could never be with him.
so naturally
i fell in love.

<u>julie</u>

she was my lover's ex
but that's not what she told me
when she started writing to me.
i guess i didn't blame her
at the time
wanting to keep him
in her life for as long as she could-
so she tried to sink her hooks in me.
i wriggled away.
so she tried other people
and they let her stay.
then she began to
slowly
      but
            surely
f
u
c
k
with our
l
i
v
e
s.
her last email to me
she called me a bitch.
well...
yeah.

٭ٯ

president

they had been friends for years,
my parents and these people.
we had gone on lake powell trips
every summer together
when i was young-
ben and sue.
when i got a little older
ben became kind of a big deal
in the mormon church.
he was called as a mission president
in scotland
and after that
he was made into a general authority
which is like a senator
in the mormon scheme of things.
so when they showed up
at my mother's funeral
everyone was so deferential to him,
calling him
president
not ben.
i was standing in a line
greeting people there to honor
my mother
and when he finally got to me
i said
thanks for coming
ben-
because that's his fucking name.
he looked insulted.
i didn't give a fuck.
we were there because of my mother-
to me
she was the important one there
and he could have just shoved his
president
up his ass
for all i cared
because
we were at a funeral-
and at a funeral
everybody's
equal.

city creek

the privileged-
shoppers meandering-
nordstrom's,
aldos,
xpress,
macy's,
lush.
the man with tan trousers
embezzled 10k when he was twenty-four
from his buddy's start-up
to buy an engagement ring
and a dishwasher for his grandmother-
the middle-aged man with jet black hair
has only one good memory about his father-
when they tied sheets around their necks
and ran around the yard
playing superheroes.
the heavy-set woman in her early fifties
skimmed money from her
grandchild's trust fund
to get botox and laser lipo-
the asian woman sits on a bench
with her blank-faced child.
she lets her husband fuck her in the ass
at night while he chokes her.
the two blondes are sisters-
one of them was bulimic in high school
and ruined her front teeth-
the other one wants a divorce
but stays for her autistic child.
the security guard walks backwards talking
on his walkie-talkie-
he had a shot
at playing college ball
but got busted for pot when he was
seventeen.
the elderly woman walking with her
broker son
remembers what it was like
to go to bed hungry
and so she made sure he never did
even after his father left
when he was nine.

the man with frizzled salt and pepper hair
dreams of fisting his daughter-in-law.
the two women on his right
are afraid of the four latino
youths lounging near the elevators.
the three business men walking briskly
through
the crowd all work at the law firm next door.
the balding one has a flask in his desk
at work.
the black man's mother
is dying of multiple sclerosis in baltimore.
the one with the belly
pays for sex
and is a sunday school teacher.
the young mother pushes her stroller
and talks on her cell phone
to her husband
who attempted suicide last year-
she never turns the ringer off.
the elderly man stands at the
cosmetic store
while the young clerk
rubs moisturizer
into his old hands.
he is remembering the touch
of his wife
who passed nine months ago.
a woman with beach curls
carries her dog with her wherever she goes
because she can't forget
the abortion she had
at sixteen.
the privileged-
shoppers meandering-
nordstrom's,
aldos,
xpress,
macy's,
lush.
they converge on a thursday
in city creek mall
and didn't know
they wore their secrets
around them like cloaks.

hungry

i used to go to this sports bar
on tuesday nights
for karaoke.
there was a doorman cum bouncer there
this black guy named
e.j.
and i flirted my ass off with him
because he was incredibly hot
and hard
and tight.
one night
i was craving sex
craving it
like this hunger
and thirst
and yearning
all balled into a fist inside me
and so i asked e.j. to come outside with me.
he bent me over
this concrete divider in the parking lot
and slammed into me from behind
because i needed to have a cock in me.
i can remember
so many times when i just needed
a fucking cock.

ॐ

record

she let him photograph
their desktop tryst.
the close-ups were
kind of fuzzy
but then so was she.
she has a pierced clit-
i never understood that
allure, really.
i wonder if she knows
where those photos are
now.

labor

with my second daughter
i got caught up in the trend of
natural childbirth.
my labor was short and intense
and i remember swearing a lot.
at one point during a particularly
painful contraction
my arm shot out
and i grabbed my then-husband
by the nipple and twisted.
had i had my wits about me
i would have grabbed much lower.

the sight

i knew this kid who
believed that with enough faith
anything was possible.
he broke his glasses,
snapped them in two
because he had faith god would heal his eyesight
and then he went hiking in
the mountains.
he came home and said
he needed new glasses.
i would have liked to have
been there when he told his religious parents
how his glasses broke.

night and day

when they were older teens
my brothers formed a two-guitar duet called
night and day.
they sang mostly folk songs
by james taylor and
harry chapin.
they played at high schools
and churches
but mostly they played
when we were all together
as a family.
they got older,
married
with kids
but every family party
they would pull out their guitars
and play and sing.
the kids and in-laws
didn't ever seem to be too interested
but other brothers, sister and parents
would sit quietly
and listen to every song
almost like we were drinking in
the moment
to fortify us
against the future.
my mom used to sit in her chair
and sway to the music
and close her eyes
as if the music filled her
in the most complete way.
i used to watch her
and i understood why
she was so reverent.
one brother is in arizona, now
the other in australia
and we don't have the gatherings
like that anymore.
i think my mom would be sad about that.
i think she wanted us all to
listen to that music
and remember
that things are constantly changing

but night and day will always be,
like the coming of spring,
like a family
who sang together
and played music
despite the fact
that we are growing older
and we are unraveling
with the passage of time.

∽∾

growing up

i can't dig my heels in
hard enough
to make this thing stop-
this growing and changing
that keeps me
grabbing my son in the mornings
and smelling his hair
covering his cheeks with kisses-
but there will come a day
when he puts his foot down
and the smothering will be over.
he left his school shoes in the hall
and where i would normally be irritated
i felt myself freeze with
an icy reality-
the shoes would almost fit me
and i stared at them in my hands
and everything sort of
ached
because
it's only a matter of time
before
those shoes
will go to
the salvation army
and he will be climbing
out of my reach,
climbing into manhood
and i will be left
with a hallway,
empty of castoff shoes
and the sound of his
voice.

birthdays

everybody ages differently.
for some people it's just a number
and for other people
it's a crisis.
they don't look at what they've gained
only what they've lost
or what they will lose.
my husband turned 50 this year
and his panic
went to levels
i couldn't understand.
i didn't know how to make him feel better
and didn't know
all of the levels
he visited
in his darker thoughts.
we drove up the road toward home
and as we went around the bend
there were about 15 young girls-
high school,
maybe college,
all running in their sports bras
and short-shorts.
i turned to him
smiled
and said
happy birthday to you.
he seemed to feel better
at least for a moment.

உ௸

home base

my brother was on the high school
baseball team
and we went to all of the games.
i had a crush on every player
except first base (he was my brother's friend
and not very nice to me)
and second base (my brother).
i especially had it for the pitcher and catcher
(who all the chicks liked, said my brother)
because they seemed like
bad boys
and from what my brother said
i knew
in some intangible way
i had something they wanted.
but i was way too young.
when i got older
the catcher
(who lived next door)
moved home
and so i made it a point
to come out and wash my car
in these slutty shorts
and a tank top.
we started talking one day
and we ended up in his basement
making out.
i found out he had lost his job
as a used car salesman
and had just got divorced.
he tried to fuck me
but i begged off
and went home.
he just didn't seem as giant
as he did
behind home plate.

ဆွေ

n.y.c/l.a.

new york city-
the cloisters at the met
gourmet rice pudding delivery
irish hunger memorial and battery park
thai food in the meat packing district
stomp off-broadway
grand central
central park
brownstones in chelsea with climbing ivy
the library hotel
nuyorican poet's café
joe's slice on carmine street
lady liberty
hot dog with peppers and onions outside the
financial district
the strand
the smell of garlic and bread in little italy
times square
street market in the village with handmade leather journals
and jewelry
the russian tea room
cabs
gotham bar and grill
women in scarves and flats
tamarinde
            los angeles-
suv drivers talking on their cells
century city and saks
frozen yogurt
starbucks.
god
i miss new york.

ూబ

kat

kat gave me her phone number.
i didn't call.
shit storm
at the lesbian bar.

mistress

my dad's old mistress
showed up
at my mom's funeral.
everyone was so polite to her
but i wouldn't talk to the bitch.
i wanted to tell her my mom died
because she had heart failure.
i wanted to tell her she'd had dementia.
i wanted to tell her she was the reason
my mom wanted to forget
and why her heart had broken.

৩৯

nyc

i remember when i got out of the terminal
and i was waiting for my bags.
everybody around me was
dark
      loud
           alive.
i remember thinking
i'm
home.

poly

there's a whole segment of the population
who identify as polyamorous.
this means they are married
to one person
but they are allowed to love
and be lovers
with other people.
i guess i can dig that.
what i don't get?
how many of them get divorced.
i mean
what's the fucking point?

* * *

pee for two

my first husband
asked me if he could pee on me
in the shower.
it was the shower
so i said he could.
so...
that happened.

partners

at the strip club
i got down in front of my boyfriend
underneath the table
attached to the stage
and sucked him off.
the dancer knew perfectly well
what we were up to.
i made him tip her a lot
because she could have told-
and i wanted to thank her
because she and i,
we had done it together.

❧

rapport

they had us pray to
heavenly father
but told us to have
a personal relationship
with jesus.
i tried
but it's hard
when they don't talk back.

parenting

my twenties and thirties
were filled with turmoil.
i think this is why i can hardly remember
the childhoods of my kids.
all i have to remember it
is who they are now.
i can see my mistakes
so clearly
and then i see how they laugh
how they think
how they need me
and i get a small glimpse into
the times when
i got it right.

༄ ༄

facing it

i was downtown today and i saw this guy
who had a severely disfigured face.
it was as though someone came up to him and wiped
all of his features all
the way over to his right side.
we sat outside
and my first instinct was to look away, so i did.
i figure
he gets enough people staring at him
and he'd appreciate being
treated
like any other person
without a fucked up face.
as i was leaving my table
he passed by again
but something made me not want to look away.
i looked at him and when his eyes met mine
i smiled and nodded to him.
he nodded back to me
and i thought that maybe he appreciated
being acknowledged
like any other person
too.

new york

i met her on a plane on my way
to new york.
she was a stewardess (flight attendant)
and she and i flirted the whole way there.
i remember getting a glimpse of her bra
over the collar of her buttoned shirt
(black and white
with lace).
i gave her my hotel info
because i was only staying the night.
it was some airport shit-hole
and while waiting for her
i watched some harrison ford movie.
she showed up at 9 pm with beer
and after two she was shirtless on the bed
and i was pulling off her pants.
she had never done this
with a woman before
she said
and so i told her i'd never done it
with a stewardess
and she got all bent that i didn't say
flight attendant.
i did it a few more times
and she got bent every time
which made fucking her
sort of fun.
the last time i did it she got
really huffy
gathered her things
and told me i was as bad as a man.
i thought the whole thing was pretty
fucking disingenuous.
she wanted to be all progressive
with the terminology
but she was still offering
coffee, tea or me.

beat

kerouac would have been
interested in me
because i'm mad.

burroughs would have been
interested in me because
my language
is a virus.

corso would have been
interested in me because
i'm unnamed.

ginsberg would have been
interested in me
because i'm holy.

mad,
unnamed,
holy,
speaking in a
viral tongue.

ৎৄৄ৲

tit for tat

one of my first mother's days.
he gave me a camp stove
for himself.
for father's day i didn't even
get him a card.
he called me petty.
i wasn't.
i was pissed.

venice

i took the bus from
wilshire avenue
to venice beach on a friday
afternoon because my boss let me leave
the office
on the 9th floor
at 3pm for good behavior.
i was sixteen and i was
in love with jim morrison
and i figured i could commune with him
in his old stomping ground
or some shit.
it was hardly the hippie paradise
i had pictured.
so many shops
and colors that
i couldn't take just one thing in
because it all hit me
like this blast of light
and sound
and voices and sweat
on people's heads
and the backs of knees.
rollerblades everywhere. muscle beach.
shops selling all the same t-shirt.
i smoked one cigarette after the other
because it was the only way
i could take in how
alive
      and
           dead
it all seemed to me.
i came to a little shop
where a middle eastern man beckoned me in.
he spoke to me in spanish
because of how tan i was.
i told him
no comprende
and he switched to english.
he held out this gauzy white dress
with white embroidery at the neck.
he told me to try it on-

really insisted that i
try it on.
i saw the dressing room
and i even saw the hole
where he peeked in
and even though i knew it would fit
i tried it on for him
in that shitty little room
with stained white walls.
it didn't feel weird
having him disappear
while i went in that room.
i felt powerful in that room.
i bought the dress
even though it was see-through.
i wore it that night without a bra
to a baskin robbins
in the simi valley suburbs
and middle-aged men stared at me
while their wives
only glanced my way.

༄

we

i had mini-bottles of jack daniels
and jim beam
in my dresser.
i drank them before school
(when i made it to class.)
debate was first
and i never went.
i always got an "a"
because my teacher wanted to fuck me.
one day i took a shot of j.d.
because it was 11 o'clock
and i couldn't miss math.
i didn't know my mom was home
from work.
i still don't know why she was home
on that particular day
because she wasn't sick
so i like to think it was because of me.
she walked into my room
without knocking
and i had the mini-bottle still in my hand.
she didn't seem surprised at all.
she just sat down on my bed
and i could suddenly feel
the weight of her world
resting on me
as she sat near me.
she stared at the floor for a long time
and then said
what are we going to do?
i didn't know how to answer her
but i really liked that she said *we*.

ড৹ঌ

monikers

two words:
pussy and cunt.
people call a weak guy a *pussy*.
people call bitchy women *cunts*.
i hate the word pussy
because it's too cute
for the power of cunt.
calling a bitchy woman a cunt
is redundant
and a compliment.

ॐॐ

understood

his wife didn't understand him
but i did.
i understood
and i understood
i understood
i understood
then she found out
i understood
and she divorced him.
he told me never
to contact him again.
in a weird way
i understood that too.

young women's

i went to young women's
for almost seven years.
it's where pre-teen and teen-aged girls
go on sundays
to learn about mormonism.
i only remember two lessons
out of those seven years.
the first was on *keeping morally clean*
a.k.a. keeping your legs closed
until marriage.
the teacher handed us all chewing gum.
we were chewing gum.
then we were supposed to unwrap it
chew it
and then spit it out.
see?
nobody wants *abc* gum.
the second lesson
was on how to properly clean your house.
you're supposed to go over
a spot with the vacuum
ten times.
ten times.
this is what i learned
as a mormon girl.
keep your legs closed
and clean your house.
this pretty much sums up
the mormon experience
for a woman.
i was always pretty good
about cleaning the house.

ৡৣ

grotesque

she was my friend
and then my room mate
and then she was nothing.
they called her gross val.
it could have been because of all the greasy make-up
she wore to cover her pock-marked face.
it could have been because she smelled like an old can
of tuna
one week out of the month.
it could have been because she had monster zits
on her ass she would pop in the mirror
(except i think i was the only one
who knew that).
maybe it was because of the constant film of
yellow goo
between her bottom teeth.
i think it's because she dressed
in the most expensive clothes
she could buy
and affected an upper-class
english accent
and thought everyone was beneath her.
she faked a degree and worked
as a high-paid graphic designer.
money came so easy to her.
i stopped thinking about her
after the time i went on vacation with her
when i was a single mother.
i brought my two daughters
to visit her in california.
on the day
we went to disneyland
i couldn't afford to buy my kids and me lunch
so i didn't eat
and i bought one kid's meal
for my little girls to share.
she bought her own lunch
and proceeded to eat
a giant piece of chocolate cake
while my hungry children
stared with
wide eyes.

angels

tennessee williams said,
if i got rid of all my demons
i'd lose my angels.
i guess i agree with that.
i just wish my angels
were a little stronger,
maybe a little more
bad ass.

ॐ

fortress

his bed was just a mattress
and box springs
and it was surrounded by a moat of
clothes
and walls of books.
the first evening i spent there
i had to tell him
he was more than
a passing thing
because i was already trapped
inside.
he seemed to take that
well.

back home

i took her to my art studio
and i taught her how to paint.
i helped her step-by-step
with a painting she called *home*.
then she moved back.
i wish i could go to her
and teach her
to paint a painting called
back there at that other place
with julieann.

৽৹৵

aunt

my aunt is 91
and her husband worked
for the rail road.
she lived across the street
from me my whole life.
she's the last of my mother's siblings,
the last of *us*.
she was stronger than my mother
so she kind of scared me
growing up
because she said exactly what she meant
and meant everything she said
and she did it with a razor tongue
and bright eyes.
she's at least a foot shorter than me now
but she still towers over me-
not because i'm intimidated,
not because she's old,
but because she taught me
who i wanted to be.

courtship

bashing my head
into the side of my car
was not the best way
for him to win back
my affections.

჻

white

we were in this
shitty little motel in
some tiny, rural college town.
it was my first time spending the whole
night with a guy.
i'd bought a matching bra and panty set
by christian dior.
they were the softest satin and
they were pure white.
i showed him my outfit
after we'd had some southern comfort
and sprite.
he laid me down on the carpet
and removed
my silken white panties.
he moved down
and buried his head into my cunt.
it was the first time for that, too.
i didn't know
my virginal white
bra and panties
would be so apropos.

cuz

what is it
about the strange allure
of first cousins?

∽≪

the threat

underneath the porch
they told me
they would get pins and needles
and stick them
in my mother's eyes
if i didn't do it.
so i squatted down and peed.
i had to go anyway.

what a feeling

i had a church teacher
who used to let me come over
and hang out all of the time.
i was 13
and didn't ever want to be home.
she lived in an apartment with
her baby daughter and her husband
who was going to pharmaceutical school.
one day i went over there
and she wasn't home.
he told me i could wait for her
because she would be back soon.
he sat close to me on the sofa
and i remember the feel
of his leg
running up the length of mine.
his hand made its way to my leg.
that night they took me to see
flashdance
and she insisted on sitting next
to me
like she knew about the couch,
like she knew about his hand and my leg.
i remember wondering
what it was about me
that made men
want to touch me
when no one was there
to say no.

alter

i miss looking at my
mother's goofy 70's-style jewelry
I miss taking the lids off
of all of her perfumes
and smelling her.

wife

i love my husband's family.
but to them
i am one dimension-
i am his
          wife.
the nice ladies
from the church tell his mother
they clip his weekly
newspaper column
and stick it
on their
refrigerators with magnets.
then we see them
at all of their religious functions
and they ask him
how's the writer?
they don't mean me.

৩৩৩

sunday

i used to drive alone
downtown on sunday nights.
i chain-smoked because
it had been church that day
and i needed my lungs filled
with something else
besides religion.

solitude

there is something surreal
about your life
when both of your parents are dead.
i feel like i'm missing these real,
tangible anchors
that tethered me to this world
and helped me know
my place in it.
there was also this unconditional love.
they were fascinated and excited
by everything i did.
when i got married again
i had two new parents,
in-laws,
and they are the greatest people
anyone could ask for.
but when something cool happens
or when i write something
i just have to share,
i can't call them.
they're not mine,
and i'm not theirs.

༒

tradition

we should not be so concerned
with the sanctity of marriage-
we should be more concerned
about the sanctity
of
love.

love

we were in the bathroom
and one guy was sucking
on my tits
while the other guy knelt
on the floor
and ate me out.
people kept pounding on the door
wanting to get in.
i wanted to tell them to
find another fucking bathroom.
i was in love.

lion's share

we were supposed to share her
but somehow he got
the bigger piece.

leonard cohen

suzanne was me
a thousand kisses deep was you
and *hallelujah* was us.
we went to see him in concert
and afterwards you made love to me
while a pipe bomb went off
in the parking lot
across the street.

❧

wall

i don't think there's a soul
alive
who could tell me
they've seen
pink floyd's *the wall*
sober.

r.m.

the joke was that all
returned missionaries were horny.
my guess is that
they were just hungry.
deprive anyone long enough
and they'll eat
the first person
who says
yes.

ৎ∽ৎ

music man

something died
the night sinatra died.
martin didn't matter
davis jr. didn't matter.
frankie mattered.
my dad used to sing a lot
of sinatra in his band-
started at fourteen and played in dance jobs
all his life.
i wondered the night sinatra died
if my dad thought about death.
i wonder if he thought
the music would just stop.

mutual friend

he accused me of trying to
ruin their friendship.
i tried to get away but
he'd jammed his fingers
up my cunt
while he held onto me
by his teeth
so i told.
the mutual friend believed him
not me.
i saw him at a bar after that
and he told me
he wanted to smash his drink glass
in my face.
when i saw him years later
he told me
he wished he had a gun
so he could blow me away.
he lives one city away from me
somewhere
and there are times
when i think about what would happen
if i saw him again.
i have dreams about him sometimes
and in the dreams
we're friends again
like
before he shoved his fingers in me
and i think i have those dreams
because
i'm just so fucking scared.

৵৶

moving on

frankly
i'm sick and tired
of the feminist
sexual-victim-centric
bullshit
poetry.
you may have been victimized
at some point-
but that doesn't mean
you have to be
and remain
a victim.

৵৶

therapy

after being married
to a cold shower personified
i found i couldn't come
with a man.
at all.
then i met this guy.
i was 26 and he was 52
and he was a psychologist.
he had an idea one night.
he told me to jack off
in his bed
while he was in the living room.
the next night
he moved closer.
then he was in the doorway.
then he was in the bed with me.
it was a break-through
i'll never forget.

religion

i was told by my well-meaning father
that believing in god
and the mormon church
was like having an orgasm.
he was trying to relate to me
but it still felt
really fucked up.

ൟൟ

ten

my daughter was about six
when she told me she wanted
a tattoo.
i didn't panic.
i asked her what she wanted and where.
she said she wanted a sunflower
on her ankle.
i told her it was
pretty expensive,
getting ink.
she seemed a little upset
so i told her i'd front her the money
and she could pay me back.
you do know how
tattooes work, don't you?
i asked.
she didn't.
so i explained the needle part,
the pain part,
the blood part.
she looked at me with wide eyes
and after a second she said,
i think i'll wait till i'm ten.

holiday

i don't know that there's
anything worse
than spending valentine's day
with someone
when there's someone else you want
to be with.
this goes for your birthday
and christmas, too.

৵৵

bad things

god doesn't stop bad things from happening.
jesus doesn't stop bad things from happening.
elohim, jehovah, allah, buddha, shiva and shakti
don't stop bad things from happening.
the goddess doesn't stop
bad things from happening.
bad things happen.

two sons

they were brothers.
both of them shot themselves
two years apart
in their parent's house.
i wonder
what they would have used
had they not received
guns
for christmas.

topless

when i was 17
i decided to lay out topless
in my backyard.
i knew no one would be home that day
so i laid out a sheet
slathered on the baby oil
and proceeded to cook.
i fell asleep in the sun
and when i woke up
i could hear voices
so i put on my glasses
and saw that the neighbors behind us
were getting a new roof.
the men were busy working
so i figured they already had
their fill of me.
i didn't cover up,
i just gathered my sheet
under my arm
and walked up the porch steps.
i wanted to maintain
what dignity i had left
by letting them think
i didn't give a shit.

wait

we were at that moment when we
couldn't wait-
it was almost painful to wait
and my insides were clenched
i stopped thinking
couldn't see straight
and so we pulled over
onto the side of the road.
we were up in the mountains
and it was dark.
the only place to go was this
big boulder
so i reclined on it
and he fucked me on the rough rock.
it was a lot less painful
than the wait in the car.

secrets

he wrote poetry
no one would see
in a journal
mingled with his religion
his doubts
his faith
his struggles
and an incomparable gift
for hiding it all
from everyone.

<u>inevitability</u>

at one point i bought into that
book/craze
conversations with god.
mine was a book on tape.
ed asner was god's voice sometimes
and ellen burstyn was god's voice
other times.
but for me
if i pictured god
he was
 ed asner.
ed said something that i took with me
since nothing else from the book
really stuck.
he said
the ultimate outcome is assured.
sometimes that thought comforts me
and sometimes it scares the living shit
out of me.
i wonder how people manage
day in and
day out
with that knowledge.
there is only one outcome.
if i were to bet on it
i'd say that most people walk around
ignoring it.
but
no matter what we do,
no matter how we live,
no matter how many friends,
or how much money,
how healthy or sick,
or how many fucking planes we
jump out of
the ultimate outcome is assured.
sometimes that thought sneaks up on me
at night
when it's quiet and dark
and i hear
my husband breathing softly
next to me.
it makes me want to roll over

and hold him tight to me
or go into my son's room
and pick him up,
cover his angel face
with kisses
or go to my daughter
and listen to her tell me
about all her grand plans.
i want to smell my granddaughter's hair
and feel her small hands turning my face
toward her-
i want to hold my oldest daughter's hand
and laugh together-
there's an ache in my chest
and it wrestles with the
peace.
on those nights
i just listen to my husband's breath,
pace my own
to his,
close my eyes
and think about all of the ways
i   can   love   them   all
every   day.

comply

i should have known
by the pictures
on his tables.
him and
a woman.
he acted like a salesman
and he was.
he sold water.
i should have known from that, too.
he served me a drink
and tried to kiss me
and i started wondering about
that drink
because everything tipped sideways
really fast.
i couldn't stand.
he was so helpful.
told me to take off my clothes
and get into his bed.
he would just hold me.
i did it
because when the world
is sideways
you need an anchor to keep you
from slipping
off of the edge
of the earth.
i did it because compliance
was still hard-wired into me.
laying in his bed
time moved slowly
and then he finally came in.
something in me clicked.
i told him i had to pee
and he waited in his bed for me while
i went to the bathroom.
with the world tilting
i dressed as fast and quiet as i could
i snuck out and through my
foggy brain remembered
my favorite leather coat in his front closet.
i grabbed my bag, ran out to my car
and cried all the way home

while the road made of terrifying leaps and turns
appeared and disappeared
from my vision.
i might have called my sister.
the next morning the world held still
again
except my head pounded
like a million trains coursed
through my temples.
i went to the computer and i typed in his address.
i told him i knew he drugged me
what he tried to do to me
and to never contact me again.
i sent him an email.
a fucking
email.

⚭

vegas

she fucked her boss
and then she sued him
for sexual harassment
because 10k
makes that kind of thing
all better.

ত৶৶

flash

becky was one of my friends
in high school
and one night
we decided to flash.
we only wore long coats-
mine was one of my dad's old
rain coats,
and we went to the local diner.
we snuck around to the big window
and when we opened our coats
the main table looking at us
was a four top
of cops.
they didn't make a move
but we ran like hell.

twitch

a civilized conversation
about violence.
it's what we were having
over wine and appetizers
my friend begged off
talking about the war
for oil he'd been in
even though i wanted to ask.
then he told us he shot a little kid
over there in iraq
and i looked at him.
his eyes went deeper than the room
and
his right cheek
just next to his nose
started twitching
like an itchy trigger finger,
like a tremor of survival.
that was all i needed to know
and all i needed to hear.
then he drank his wine
and we were all civil again.

ক্ষ

tripping

there are times
when you hallucinate
when you know
you're just hallucinating.
then there are the other times.

preaching what you practice

my brother is a mormon.
he's one of three of my brothers
who are still believers.
he got called to serve
as a mission president in australia.
i wasn't going to see him for three years
so i went to his house before he left
to say goodbye.
he did something
i guess i should have expected-
he asked me how i lost my faith.
i figured it was his last push to clean house
before he went out
to clean house in australia.
we talked for two hours
and he had no problem telling me
how wrong i was-
about everything church related.
he pointed his finger at me
wrong, wrong, wrong-
but i felt really peaceful.
the more peaceful i felt
the more agitated he seemed to get.
there were so many ways
i could have fucked with his faith-
so many contradictions i could have pointed out,
but i didn't.
i just let him be who he was
and i let him think he was right
because in the end
my job is to accept him
and love him anyway.
that's what his church teaches
so i'm not sure
how he missed that.

ھو

the tango

everyone blamed dad.
the fights
the yelling
the low self-esteems
the total and complete chaos.
but i watched my mom
pretty close
and she fought back
and she fought dirty
dirtier than he did.
they split them up
into *sinner* and *saint*.
but i saw her sins
against him
watched her chip away
at the tiny amount of self-regard
he had.
when she told me once
i was just like him
after she learned i wasn't a virgin
dad and i had something in common
after that.
she chipped away at me too.
those two tangoed
and no one was blameless.
but they still blame it all
on him
as if he carried the banner
of conflict
all on his own.
as if he didn't get his verbal beatings
while they
danced in their constant raging
and discord
together.

❧

conflict

i'm in conflict about what i did
or in this case
didn't do.
my mom was in a home-
assisted living
and she was forgetting.
i saw her all the time
but many of the visits ended
with me in the car
in tears.
she wasn't herself
and to know her when she was herself
was to seriously mourn the loss.
she was vibrant and playful
and it was she who got down on the floor
to play with the grandchildren.
so when she was losing who she was
i didn't take my kids to see her
because i didn't want them to remember her
like that.
i wanted them to remember her as she was before-
larger than life
filled with love and wonder and
child-like vitality.
i remember the day i visited her
and she introduced me to another
resident as
her favorite niece.
i spared my children that.
i don't know what they would have come away with
had she forgotten who they were.
so they didn't see her much
and then she died.
they talk about her
as that larger than life
figure
and i think i did
the right thing.
but then i think about
their last time holding her
and hearing her say
that she loved them
and no matter who she thought

they were
she would have told them that.
then i'm conflicted
all over again.

ֆe⌐

higher being

i used to believe in the
judeo-christian god and thought
that everything i did was
watched
like some dime store creeper
getting off
on my sins.
anything good happened
it was because of him;
anything bad happened
it was because i didn't believe enough
in *him*.
later i transferred my beliefs to
pagan gods
because what's further away from
god the father
than goddess the mother?
she was much easier to deal with
because she wasn't concerned
about sins
just about
right thinking.
but i don't do that so hot either.
but it was fun thinking
everything was magical and doable
with the right colored candles
and essential oils
and fucking rocks
as if rocks
vibrated
or some shit.
and i remember when i was single
and alone
with three kids
and the wishful thinking
and magic
and rocks
just didn't seem to be working,
and so i gave it all up.
everything and everyone.
gave up on everyone
but me.
suddenly

things started falling into place
and it wasn't because of *him*
and it wasn't because of *her*
it was because of me.

❧

sins

they go to church on sunday
and the gym on monday
to make up for their
sins
on saturday.
unsanctioned fucks on
non-nuptual beds
pork rinds
tequila
taco bell
and so they do penance
american style.

၄ၕ

retrospect

why is it that
        men
can't decide they don't
        want
to be with you until
                after
they've fucked you?

the game

my husband plays rugby.
when he's out on the field
a sort of dark film
covers his face,
his eyes look blood-hungry
and a dangerous
vibration
sears through his body-
i can feel it when he comes to get water
from me
on the sidelines.
i like this part of him
this
male
power
violent
aggressive
           dominant
              virile
part of him
because all of those parts of him
come out
when he fucks me
and it feels
like i'm the spoils of war.

∾

wanted

she was my best friend.
she and her boyfriend were 19
i was 16
and i went with them to a party.
he couldn't stop staring at me
and on the way home we all sat
in the front seat.
he had his arm around my friend
but his hand was brushing
along my shoulder
and cheek.
somehow he got my number
and called.
i let him pick me up
and we went to his dad's furniture store.
i lost my virginity to him
on a brown leather couch.
he was my friend's boyfriend
and i should have known better
but i remember back then
feeling so hungry
for love
so hungry to be wanted.
it sort of eclipsed any sense of
morality
and it did for a really long time.
i just needed to be wanted.
if they fucked me
they wanted me
and that meant
that i wasn't as bad
as all that.

ဆ

absent

i hadn't seen him in weeks.
he didn't write or call
so when he showed up at my party
in a suit
fresh from his brother's wedding
he was the only guest that mattered.
we shot tequila rose
into each other's mouths
and it looked like
the kiss of life.
even though people were there
i left and went to the bedroom with him
because when he was around
i couldn't stay out of the bedroom.
we tore at each other's clothes
and at one point i hit him
and cried
because he'd been so gone.
he got on top of me
and as he fucked me he said
i fucking love you.
his ear was close to my mouth
and i was still crying
so i asked him
where have you been?
he didn't answer
he just told me
as he fucked me
that he wanted to fuck the world with me.
i didn't tell him that
he was my world
and so to me
that was redundant.

৵৵

pins

in high school
i called myself an atheist.
i even had a button in my car
with the word *god* crossed out.
my friend knew better and figured
i was just pissed at being raised
a mormon
so she gave me another button
that read
how much sin can i get away with
and still go to heaven?

✂

hysterical patriots

i was too young
to remember orson wells
and the war of the worlds
mass hysteria.
but people
and their shitty common sense
has remained faithful
with fear of a black president
a woman in charge of her own body
the need for personal arsenals
and the fear of immigrants
living in the land of the free.
but
we are only as free
as our fear,
so from where i sit
we're a nation of indentured
fucking servants
working to pay off history.

summer job

in the summer
i was a pool attendant
at a condo complex.
it was me, one other girl
and three guys.
there was an older guy named mike
who lived there
and he was a pool attendant too.
one night we hot-knifed hash
over his stove
with an empty toilet paper roll
and then he and i fucked in his dark bedroom
and only when we were fucking
did i realize
how weird it was for
some 25 year old guy
to work as a pool attendant with a bunch of
17 year olds
and so
i didn't fuck him again.
and summer was over
just like that.

৩৯

the ride

he laid prostrate
on the filthy black floor
while a nude woman
slithered her body over him.
she ground herself on him
until he came.
all the while his family
was at disneyland
riding entirely different rides.

pavlov

mormon courtship
does not favor the mormon male.
they used to send young men of 19
into the mission field
to preach the mormon gospel.
that gave the young men a chance to go
to college for a year.
they'd meet a nice girl.
they would date
and all of those heady
sexual feelings
were just bubbling
ready to burst from him.
then he gets called to serve his mission
and she says she'll wait for him.
she sends letters
care packages
and when he gets home
she's there,
waiting,
like an eager puppy.
they let themselves be alone
they make out and his hand wanders
over her ass
and suddenly
he's in love.
and she promises him
with her body
that the insatiable thirst
he has raging inside
will be forever quelled
if he promises to marry her
for eternity.
eternity.
as if people at the age of 22
know what they want
for that fucking long.
he proposes and the wedding's on.
he doesn't know
he's going to be at her whim
for the rest of his life.
he doesn't know she holds
what's in between her legs

as his pavlov's reward
for good behavior.
they hoodwink those boys
so good
you'd think it was
women who controlled
the mormon church.

৵৵

sticky

his ex was like dog shit
you can't get off of your shoe.

❦

jean

by 17 i knew how to handle my liquor.
we were all on the same floor
of the hotel
by cal state fullerton
on a debate trip.
i was in a room with three senior guys
and a junior, like me
but she was completely-fucked-up.
i told her she needed to come with me
but she wanted to stay with the guys.
i talked to her
and talked to her
i even grabbed her arm
but she wouldn't leave
so i left her there
with the three of them.
they passed the polaroids
around on the bus
on the trip home.

gesture

i worked with this girl
who used to cut herself.
they called it a *gesture*.
i called it a 9-1-1
fucking emergency.

৩৵

stud

he was way too young for me,
just out of the service
and he could play darts.
i was a pool player.
he was tall and had a stud
in his tongue that he hid
from everyone,
even when he was stationed in haiti.
he didn't have a car or a place of his own
so he had me drive him
to his parent's house to fuck me.
we watched a movie
and when his little bitchy sister
wouldn't leave us alone
we went to his bedroom.
he was tall and it was
a good time
fucking in his little boy's
narrow bed.
he went down on me
and i was excited to feel that stud
but it didn't make
a bit of difference.

string theory

I dated some guy who wouldn't fuck me
when i had my period.
my first husband didn't like to either.
the guy said it was disturbing to see
blood all over his cock
and i thought about his fears.
did he knick himself shaving down there
as a boy?
did he de-flower a virgin
in a particularly bloody fashion?
what could be scary about blood.
i wondered if it was me
because that blood was me
a literal part of me
he rejected.
some years later
in a much anticipated tryst with a man
in a hotel room
i waited until the last possible second
meaning we were naked,
ready to go,
and i told him i had my period.
he didn't say anything to me.
he reached down,
found the string to my tampon
and pulled it out,
throwing it across the room.
problem solved
he said.
it's why i married him.
at least, that's my theory.

ౡ∘ಳ

the ranch

i knew this guy who
got divorced
and he was pretty desperate
for physical touch.
he could have probably
gone out with some woman
and fucked her
but it's never that simple
and when your head is fucked up
from divorce
the last thing you need
is an entanglement
with someone else
who's probably fucked up
from a divorce.
he drove to nevada
and went to a whorehouse.
they lined the women up
so he could choose which one
he would fuck.
he chose an older women
who seemed kind
as opposed to some younger,
hotter chick in the line.
she was very professional
and he was right about one thing-
she was kind.
she got on top of him
and rode him like a pro
and he was done fast.
he paid her
and it was over.
you've got to compare that
to asking someone out,
making small talk at dinner,
the awkward first kiss
on her couch,
and waking up the next morning
with all of her expectations
crowding you
right out of her bed.

the pack

there were about twenty girls
in our group
but only about four approached me
in the lunchroom.
i was in seventh grade
and i was finally in with the
popular crowd.
but it didn't last
because friendships for me
never did.
we hate you.
that's what the girl told me
and i knew that
we
meant
all.
everything changed
after that.
i missed a lot of school
that year.
i became dependent on
the outcasts
who were unaware
that i was
the social pox.
it got better
because these things always do
and by ninth grade
i was
voted in as a cheerleader
by a popular vote
(not skill)
those girls were nice to me then-
but i never forgot.
i still get
 nervous
in groups of women.
i still brace
for the blow
at our nice
grown-up lunches
and our after dinner
drinks.

immersion

i was baptized a mormon
when i was eight.
according to everyone
i reached the age
of accountability.
i want to know
who was accountable
for everything
i did
because i was
baptized at eight.

৩৵৶

license

people who believe
in god
seem to give themselves license
to do everything
god says not to.

sunday morning
church service

row 2, aisle-
her mother told her she would never
be pretty
but she could choose to be kind.
row 4, end-
she is self-conscious now
because people can see
her scalp through her
white hair.
row 5, aisle-
he wants to have one more child
and she is so afraid that
this time she will die.
row 6, middle-
her mother warned her the
other members would judge her if she
put that pink streak
in her hair.
row 9, end-
she hasn't spoken to her father
in three years because she has a false
memory that
he molested her.
row 10, middle-
he is having an on-line affair
with an old girlfriend
from high school.
row 13, aisle-
he is a racist and secretly avoids
the latino family who live
four doors down
and sit in front of him.
row 16, end-
he can no longer see
the words to the hymns
so he pretends to sleep
during the songs.
row 17, middle-
she is secretly in love
with their sunday school teacher.
row 21, aisle-

they are always late for church
because their adhd child
causes them to fight
before meetings.
row 24, middle-
she prays to be rid of the envy
she feels
for her wealthy sister
and resents how happy she is-
belief masquerading as knowledge-
façades masquerading as perfection-
fear masquerading as faith-
the worshipping mass
breathes in unison
while their lives
s l o w l y
d i s i n t e g r a t e.

story

once when i was fourteen
i got fingered
on a church lawn.
that's it
fingered.
church lawn.

❧

rest

i could hear the band
practicing at the stadium.
i was smelling my cat's fur
and trying to think of one good reason
to get up besides
coffee and nicotine.

timber

he lavished affection on the dog,
but he was also cruel.
her name was timber and when
i married him
she became my dog too.
she was a black lab-german shepherd mix
and she could do this trick
where she would jump up
and remove a guy's baseball cap
with her teeth.
after i left him
she'd pee every time she'd see me
like she was being punished.
she eventually ran away from him, too.
i was lucky.
she was hit by a car on i-215.
i tried to tell him-
the moments of cruelty
would always outshine
the affection.
he wouldn't lose anyone
or anything
unless they didn't want to get lost.

ഏഝ

the past

no one can resist
the pull of nostalgia
especially
in the bedroom.
the old girlfriend from
high school
you only got to feel up,
the lover from your twenties
who first did you from behind,
the childhood friend
who knew your parents.
shared backgrounds,
instant intimacy
usually ending
in disaster.

flirt

something happens
when you hit forty-
at least it did for me.
i realized i stopped flirting.
i've seen older women flirt
and it's not pretty.
it's like they don't realize
the cute
twenty-something waiter
has options
besides
a middle-aged woman
and it always looks a tad pathetic.
i'm careful at bars, too
because you add alcohol
into the over-forty-flirt-mix
and it just gets tragic.
so today
some guy at a department store
asked me to help him decide
on some shirts—you know, colors—
the gray one, the blue and yellow one…
he was probably my age
grey eyes
nice smile
and i found myself
taking out that flirty part.
it took a second to get it warmed up
and it felt a little awkward
trying it on
but once i got it out
it felt really good.
i became aware of my eyes
and smile again
aware of living inside
this body of mine
and feeling like an autonomous
sexual being-
a separate sexual energy
not involving my husband.
the guy had parked right next to me
and smiled and waved at me
as we pulled out.

i checked my lipstick
in the mirror.
i couldn't wait to
get in bed with my husband
and tell him
how i'd felt-
like i'd had a depth charge
alive
and aware
that i can still turn a head or two
even if it's only
for my excellent sense
of color.

prom

this guy tried to fuck me
to ravel's *bolero* once.
i just started laughing
and i couldn't stop

∽∾

ruthless

his dad owned smith's
grocery store
and he was in my apartment on the floor
while i was grinding on him.
we still had our clothes on
and i came really hard.
you're ruthless
he said.
he'd had no idea.
i stopped answering his calls
after that.
i had other shit to do
besides
stupefying
little rich boys.

power

the whole bdsm thing.
i knew a woman who was into it.
she was submissive.
a submissive.
she was involved with a married couple
who were dominant
and their idea of being dominant
was to make her wear a dog collar
and spend time
in a giant dog kennel.
then she met me.
i understood the whole thing
on a different level
that had nothing to do with costumes
and being called *mistress*.
i told her she didn't have to wear a collar
she never had to go in a kennel
and i would never mistreat her.
then i said
but i am dominant to you.
do you understand?
she did.

⤞⤝

the driver

he had a black ear
and neck
and a bushy beard to hide
all of that black.
soft voice and eyes.
he was reading ayn rand
and told me that
china
was taking over everything.

home

when i was younger
i was a practicing mormon.
i used to love to go to
the mormon temple.
you sat through a movie about adam and eve
and how everything was created
and satan was a guy
not a snake.
after the movie
you made promises and
did secret handshakes
and all this symbolic shit
before you were allowed to
progress to the next room
which was the room
god lived in.
it was called
the celestial room.
it was always mostly white
with soothing colors
and gold
and soft, holy music
piped in.
there were chairs everywhere
to sit in and feel god,
feel what it was going to be like
living with him.
i always wanted to stay in that room
forever
when i first got in
because it was so peaceful-
it was supposed to be like how our
eternal home would be after we died.
it buzzed
with this electric feeling
brought on by
the collective group
all murmuring in each other's ears
reverently
and probably the music.
but then there came a point where
i couldn't take it
anymore

and i wanted to leave,
be done with it.
we'd leave the temple
and we were back in the dirty
shitty
foul
crass
world
with all of its imperfections.
the noise of traffic
the unhappy faces of suffering people
the old men crying
and the jay-walking freaks
who caused blasts of car horns.
it was a stark contrast
to that quiet, peaceful room
but i felt more at home in the world
than in heaven.

∽∾

the job

i used to work for
child services
for the state.
i took kids away from their parents
because their parents were abusive
or had abusive boyfriends
or refused to protect them
from sexual abuse.
but the kids didn't understand any of that
shit
they just wanted their mommies.
i was also in charge of their visitation
with their parents.
i had to just sit there while this mom told
her little 8 year old son
she was giving him away.
he was a tow-headed blond
who quietly cried all the way back
to his foster home.
once i had three little girls in the back of
my car
screaming
because we'd left their mom at visitation
and they wanted to stay with her.
it was christmas time
so while they screamed for their mom
i sang christmas carols
really loud
to try and get them to join in 'jingle bells'.
i had to pull over after i dropped them
back to their foster home.
even though i was going home
to my kids
all safe and sound,
i was really fucked up.

ॐॐ

surprise

the father
peeked in on her
in the shower.
that dissonance
between who she was
and what she was.
it's hard-wired into
the male brain.
why are
we so surprised?
outrage
and hypocrisy
living in one person
one house
one culture.
we shouldn't be
surprised by anything
anymore.

p.j.'s

it was a pajama party
for grownups.
after we wished the guest of honor
a happy birthday
we went to our car
and he thought it would be
a fun idea to fuck me against
the passenger-side door.
people kept coming into the party
walking right past us
and i decided
we were there to remind them
that it was a pajama party
for grownups.

decisions

i said
     no
more than i said
       yes-
does that still make
me a slut?

୬ஐ

oblivious

we were in one bed
and his brother
was in the other.
we thought he was
asleep
but i secretly hoped
he wasn't.

no

i once spent the night
in a bathtub.
the guy i fucked
was in the next room.
the guy who wanted to fuck me
was in there too.
he didn't like the word no.

❧

the bard

we sat around
this group of strangers-
some had books
others had sheets of paper
and some used their phones
or a laptop.
we were all poets.
we were there to read our shit.
the blue collar guy sat next to me
and i guessed he was there
to get laid
like the other guy i knew there.
he'd been coming on to me
on chat all week.
but the blue collar guy
he pulled out his poem
and he read
and his voice was scratchy and unsure.
i listened
and listened again
and as if some hand came up,
i suddenly choked on his words
in the best possible way.

sobriquets

babe
hun
sweetheart
honey
darling
doll
sweets
why is it that women reject
all of these monikers-
unless they're coming
from a gay man
getting us a perfume sample
or a martini?

❧

shit

we read poetry with each other.
nobody gets my shit.
he tells me he loves the way i smell
and then i sit and read poetry alone.

roxanne

my dad picked out my first car.
i'd wanted the neighbor's fiat
but instead he bought me
a tan ford escort
with shitty brown stripes
down the sides.
my car payment was $79 bucks a month.
he gave me a quick lesson
in manual transmission.
later that day i drove with my friend to
holladay oil to buy a pack of cigarettes.
that was the place to go because
they didn't card.
when i went out to start the car
it wouldn't start.
my friend told me i had to name the car
or it wouldn't start
so i picked *roxanne*
because that was the song on the radio.
she started right up
and i lit a cigarette
and we drove down highland drive
with the windows down
and with her name purring
in the engine
like a mantra.

∽∾

<u>kneel</u>

he said
you've done it before
but that didn't mean
i would do it again
so i told him
to get his fucking hand
off my fucking head.

treasure

my mom complained
that my dad was a pack rat.
i used to go through his drawers
to see what she meant.
he had an old cap gun
that still smelled of gun powder.
the drawers smelled like something musty
and certs
and a little bit like english leather.
there was a magnifying glass
pill bottles with
quarters neatly stacked inside.
rubber bands, newspaper clippings
of old friends who had died.
he had a view finder
a really old camera
a harmonica
and slides.
his baton to lead the choir was in there
and old, half-opened packages of candy.
a mini-stapler
little notebooks
with hand-written sayings.
it was like a treasure chest
of loot
and i would give just about anything
to have one of those drawers
here, now
intact.

ॐ

evolution

it was a dry spell
brought on by too many
meds.
i couldn't do anything-
write
paint
snap
fuck.
i went to my doctor
and told him
i thought maybe it was some
hormonal shit
but he suggested to me
that i was *evolving*.
into what?
i thought
a fucking rock?

လွာ

fathers

i watched
as one father sat with his generously
chested daughter at a table
while another father walked by
with his long-legged, nubile
daughter
both fathers checking out
each other's little girls.

string

at some point
my cats installed a
pull-string
in my back.
whenever i see them
they pull it
and all sorts of
ridiculous shit
comes out of my mouth.

❧

pie

on thanksgiving
we surprised the kids
with the newest
harry potter video
and we would settle down
in the living room
and eat pumpkin pie
and watch.
my whole world was in that room-
all of the comfort and love
and contentment
wrapped up
in a movie
and children
and pie
and him.
the only thing in common
finally was the movie
and him-
they were both filled with illusions.

faith

i remember when i lost my faith.
parts of it were gradual
and parts of it were
as sudden as a lightning storm.
parts of it were unconscious
and others were so clear
i could see
all the way
to the edge of the earth.
i'd bought my last vial of snake oil
and i was ready
to try some coffee
and fresh air.

৶৶

atlas shrugged

he told me there was no such thing
as a selfless act.
altruism
is an illusion.
i told him that
even if selfishness
is a motivation
it doesn't take away from an act
of humanity.
i guess it just depends
on where you want to shine
the spotlight.

knowing

i didn't know
my body could do that.
a lot of women do it
but at 20
i didn't watch much porn
featuring women
who could squirt.
we had only been married
a little while
and we were still
a little wild
so we went to a lookout
over the valley
and he went down on me
on the hood of his
ugly
red, yellow and blue
painted honda
as if that wasn't just asking
for a cop's attention.
when i came
it was like a fountain
and he jumped back
wiping his mouth
and yelled at me
told me i peed in his mouth.
i held back from then on
and i stopped coming
altogether
because i didn't know
what other things my body could do.
i was right, though.
his car was a cop magnet
and the fucker got pulled over
a couple of times every month.
it was something i knew
would happen
it was a time when things
stopped surprising me
because when i jacked off
in the bathroom alone
after he'd fuck me
i would squirt
and i knew
i wasn't peeing.
i knew so much shit he didn't know after that.
it's why i left.

hell

i thought i was a lesbian
for a long time when i was a teenager.
as a mormon girl i kind of thought
i was going to hell
but i couldn't help it because
boys kind of grossed me out.
i finally got into boys
but the girl thing never quite
went away.
in my twenties i dated a guy
who told me i could like both
and it was okay.
for some reason
i stopped worrying about hell
after that.

ം⌖ം

men

sometimes i wonder
what it would be like
to have a cock.
i could adjust it
play with it
feel it
grope it
any time i wanted.
then i realize that
i have tits
and i totally get it.

mormon boys

there is no such thing
as a 'good mormon boy'.
i know
because i went out with one
of the best ones.
he was buddy-buddy
with our religion teacher
at school-
that kind of teacher
who tries to be one of the
guys
and cool
and not like a grown up.
we went to dinner
and then to his fancy house
in the fancy part of town
down to his dark basement
to watch a video.
he started kissing me
and then he tried to
take off my shirt.
i don't know if he did that
with every girl he took out
or if it was just me
because of the way people
saw me at school
which was a
s
     l
         u
            t
but i didn't let him do it.
it wasn't because i wasn't into it.
it was because he thought he could
and i thought *fuck that*.
he took me home
before the movie ended.
never asked me out again,
incidentally.
my ostensible purity
notwithstanding
he must have told his friends
and his buddy-buddy teacher
he got in my pants.
the teacher treated me different after that
and that really pissed me off
because i didn't do
fucking anything.

judgment

i dated a nice mormon man
who i was trying
(rather successfully)
to corrupt.
coming up the stairs
i overheard my dad telling
my mom
that he hoped i could snag this guy
on account of his good
mormon-ness and all.
my mom told my dad i didn't
deserve him.
i remember thinking
what the fuck is wrong with you?
you're my fucking mother.

ᔕᗢᔐ

blame

i wasted all of my
outrage on my fucking religion.
it should have been wasted on god-
cut out the middle man.

crown colony

my brothers played baseball
at the local community league.
i went to every game
and i would go underneath the bleachers
with a box
gathering litter
because if i filled that box
i got a free sno-cone.
it was like this other world
under the bleachers
and i caught snippets of conversation
and adults
saying bad words
and clandestine plans being made
by teenagers
and it made gathering the litter
like this magical quest.
i wanted that sno-cone
but i took my time
because i mostly remember
desperately wanting
something to happen to me.
i wandered underneath the bleachers
yearning for my life
to begin.

୶ஓ

head

i dated a guy who hated fucking.
all he wanted me to do
was blow him.
he did the same for me
but
it's just not the same
as fucking.
all that mattered to him was
his cock
in my mouth.
when i'd suggest we fuck
he acted all reluctant
and butt hurt.
i guess he actually needed me
like a hole in the head.

biting

after we had sex on the couch
my boyfriend looked down at his
underwear
and there was blood.
it wasn't mine,
it was his.
my cunt has teeth.

sickbed

his mother had to have a nurse
come in every day.
the nurse was twenty-eight and
married
to an abusive prick.
she had to teach him
how to manage his mother's care
at night
when she left.
he was only nineteen.
one afternoon
while his mother slept
he fucked the nurse
on the dining room floor.
she came to the funeral
with her husband.
he wanted to talk to her
and tell her
that she'd made it all
bearable
but she left
before he could say goodbye.

joy

she's filled with anger
and self-loathing
because she's overweight.
her company is blackmailing her
to lose
and she hates the diet
and she hates herself
for hating the diet.
her mind works
in the most extraordinary of ways
and her history
is a volume of
color and sound
and no one sees the world
like joy sees the world-
and i marvel at that
and at her-
so why can't she see herself
the way i see her
and love the beauty
she embodies
when she lights
the room on fire?

ళౢఞ

mad river

there was the greg i fooled around with
the greg i joked around with
and the greg i wanted to fuck.
at the end
all three gregs hated me
because of adam.
adam loved me
but i didn't love him back.

৽৵

summer

i set up a pool
in the back yard
the kind with hard edges
and cartoon fish on it.
there was a toddler slide
that i stuck in it
and my little girls would slide in the pool
and scream
while i sat in my bathing suit
and watched.
the days never seemed to be
as hot as they are now.
my oldest daughter
talked the littler one into going in face-first
and she got a mouth and nose
full of water
and cried.
i pulled her up and held her
and she looked at me
and told me there was
a halo around my head.
i told her
she just had water in her eyes.

hand-out

when we get to the 4th south exit
there is always at least one or two
people begging
at the stop light.
one guy had a stroller and a sign that read
single dad please help.
you couldn't see the kid because it was
covered with a blanket
which frankly, seemed a bit odd in 90 degree weather.
another guy waved a sign saying
god bless you
and another
have a great day and smile!
but the guy i was most inclined to help
didn't have a sign.
he was in these blue dungarees
with dirty hair
and a tangled, sun-bleached beard
and he was there on the side of the road
dancing.
he just danced
and danced
and his dancing
seemed to encompass
all of the signs
that i'd ever read before.

❦

eleven

i met him at a fund raiser.
he was raising money for his
olympic bobsled team.
i was wearing a shirt
that showed off my belly
and a long floral skirt
that left what was below
a swaying, flowery
gauzy mystery.
i danced for him
because he was the captain
of the team
and you could tell he was
by the way he sat in the middle
and the way
his eyes commanded the rest.
we met in the alley out back
and i gave him a hand job
because the team bus was waiting.
eleven years later
at his book signing
i showed up
and he was still wondering
what was underneath that skirt.
we went to a hotel and he found out
and told me he'd been dreaming of me
for eleven years.
i didn't know if it was a line
or if he meant it
but i made sure
that every dream
from those eleven years
was worth it.

∞∞

news

my mom was ironing
an endless pile of shirts
when she saw
jfk get shot on t.v.
my husband was sent home
from his job at the airport
on september 11.
he turned on the news and we watched
before i drove my daughters
to school.
i listened on the radio
in the car
and i looked at the woman
in the car next to me
and she was crying
too.

❧

legal age

nobody used to card.
it was so easy getting a drink
but especially in
san francisco.
i didn't have a debate match
until 3
and so i went down to the hotel bar.
i tried to look
sophisticated
as i ordered by bloody mary.
at 16 i must have looked
something like an adult
because he gave me the drink
plus a side car.

ghost of christmas past

i don't remember how old i was
but i still wore those keds shoes
with the round toes.
i was walking home in the dark
with my mom
after a church christmas party.
she worked with all the kids in
primary
and they all loved her
but they all seemed to hover around her
afterwards like
needy little ghosts.
it was the holidays
so i talked and talked about what i wanted
santa to bring me
and my mom was so tired
and stressed
(i get that now)
and so she said
oh, you know there isn't a santa.
i remember i sort of stopped breathing
and for her sake i pretended that i did know
but my mind raced to every gift
from every christmas before
and the magical disappearance
of carrot bread and egg nog on christmas eve
and i didn't let her see me cry.
i stopped talking
(which is all she probably wanted)
and i pretended everything was fine
but i remember feeling like
someone had died.

ৎৄৎ

what if

a girl i went to high school with
just lost her husband to cancer.
she wrote about it on facebook.
she said they weren't mourning
because he was home with his heavenly father
and they'll see him again.
i can see why people
go to church.
when someone says it
with such conviction
you can almost believe it to be true.
what if?
what if?
so i don't say anything
because i have my own convictions
and they're shitty bleak
and nothing like a hopeful reunion
and angels
and a tunnel of light.
and what if i'm right?
what if?
what then?

ை‍ஐ

dark

i had never done it before
and i wanted to try.
we'd been listening to
pink floyd's
dark side of the moon
so we found a dark side of the park
and the grass was wet.
i knew enough to figure out
what felt good
and he seemed to like
what i was doing so i bobbed
my head up and down
and was so focused
i didn't hear the two dogs
approach us
in the dark.
someone was out for a late
night walk.
the dogs came over
and he covered his cock
and not me
and i felt completely exposed
even though
there were no lights.

cuervo

the only time he felt the buzz
was when he shot tequila.
then something took over him
that made him take over me
so i always encouraged
the tequila thing.

∽∾

lies

my friend johnny went to prison
because some chick he'd been dating lied
about getting beat up.
it made me think about all of the women
who get beat up
all of the women who lie
and then there's those of us who
see their attackers
at their daughter's wedding.
he never got jail time
and our daughters
forget.

grownups

there were some kids in the
neighborhood
who i couldn't play with because
their parents didn't like me.
it's weird when you're a kid
to know
that grownups don't like you.
it makes you curious
about what kind of power you have
that makes them so afraid.

∽∾

culpable

i was told my dad fucked around
on my mom
with many of her close friends.
they said he was persuasive
and charming.
i can't help but think
that her friends had something
to do with it too.

peaches

i was dressed like a hippie
in my tie-dye shirt and levis
but everyone else
had safety pins and shit in their faces.
billy rat had a blue mohawk
and he was slamming
in the middle of the room with
two other guys. one was named t.j.
there was a bare bulb hanging from the ceiling
and black flag was playing really loud
and i just tried to not get hit
by flailing limbs.
my friend jennifer
had a sort of mohawk
but it stopped just on the top of her head
and it was at least a foot tall.
people nicknamed her peaches
because she let t.j. stick some canned peaches
in her cunt
and eat them out.
we walked to the indian cultural center
and saw the descendants play in concert
but i left early
to lie on the grass because i was sick.
it was cold
because it was november and some guy
in a vw asked me if i needed a ride home.
he drove me all the way back
to the suburbs and dropped me off
at my house.
i can't believe i lucked out
and didn't get some rapist.
i walked in and it was late
and my dad saw me
but i ran to the bathroom to puke.
when i came out he had made me chicken noodle soup.
i remember he said *happy birthday* to me
because it was my birthday and i
was eighteen.
he pretended not to smell the smell
of cigarettes and puke.

છ૮૭

walgreens

that place you stop off
because the door is closer to
your parking spot
than the grocery store.
and i was looking up the aisle
when i saw this skinny woman
with her two skinny kids.
i remember how bony her shoulders
were in her tank top
the tattoo on her arm
that looked half-done and when the boy
knocked a bottle of dish soap on the floor
she grabbed his arm and yanked him to her
and called him
stupid.
he looked cross and whined
and she told him to stop
screwing around
and i wondered how many times
she'd called him names
and if the grown man in him
would believe her
or if he would believe in himself.

∞∞

cold

we started bar hopping
at 10pm.
we knew the owner of one bar
and the big-time sports caster
was there and he felt me up.
we ended up at the bar owner's house
doing shots of goldschlager and
aftershock and avalanche and i
suddenly got really cold.
i was with a guy named tal
and he didn't seem to care
how fucked up i was
so i went to the bathroom
and took a hot shower.
tal's friends seemed concerned
because they kept coming into the
bathroom and opening the shower curtain
to see if i was okay.
one of them stole my panties
and i think it was the bar owner.
tal and i stopped dating
after that.

clap

i learned my lesson the hard way.
you should never fuck someone
because they remind you of someone else.
but that's why i fucked brad.
it was a seedy business in a car
in a dark parking garage.
he wasn't like the other guy at all
but both of them
had fucked this chick
who had chlamydia.
she and i later became friends
bound by a shared cock
but we weren't bound by the clap.
i didn't get it.

charlie

his name was charlie
and that's what i called him
but he wanted everyone
to call him chazz.
we played pool together at the local
pub
and he was my friend
even though he saw me as more.
he had red hair and a red beard
that made him look like a giant leprechaun
which was funny because that was
the name of the bar.
he traveled a lot
for work
and one night when i'd drank too much
we went to his place
and he fucked me
on his immaculate bedroom floor
with no socks on it and
a suitcase in the corner.
he gave me his phone number
and i gave him mine but i
never returned charlie's calls.
when i saw him at the bar again
he acted like a little bitch,
all butt-hurt and angry.
he treated me different then
so i started calling him chazz.

meta4man

i know a guy who can sense things.
i don't believe in all of that shit
but i can tell you--
this guy knows his shit.
when i look at him
his skin seems to be made out of
one huge nerve
and it vibrates
with the slightest shift
in the atmosphere.
he loves horses
and he loves people
and then what i see in him
are the things he's lost.
he searches through
this third eye
and sees people's pain
and i wonder if he doesn't wish
he could just turn it off,
just say
fuck it
i'm a giant callous
and nothing can touch me.
but then
i asked him
what his epitaph would be
and he couldn't answer me.
but i don't think it ever crossed his mind
to simply not care,
to shut down,
to not love.
i don't know why
that isn't his
epitaph.

friends

i hung around connie and jen
but like most of my friends
historically
they proceeded to cast me off
because i was too fucked up.
not that they weren't,
but my particular brand of crazy
leaned toward the
misanthropic.
they smoked a lot of weed
and they dropped acid
and i wasn't into messing with my mind
in that way
so we drifted apart
even though connie and i had been
real close for a while.
i saw connie 8 or 9 years after graduation
and when you've had shit happen in school,
after you get out it's all bygones
so i was happy to see her and i said hi.
she looked at me and there wasn't any light
of recognition in her eyes
when she saw me.
she said my name
but her eyes
seemed focused on a point
through my face
and on the back of my skull
like i needed to wave my hand
in front of her.
it was weird
because she was gone.

∽∾

newborn

when i had my first baby
she wouldn't breastfeed.
she was five weeks early
and really, really small
and all she would do was latch on
and then fall right to sleep.
i was depressed
and if i couldn't even feed my own baby
what good was i going to be
for all the other shit i needed to do?
i tried telling my husband
about my feelings
and he got all freaked out and asked me
if i wanted to hurt her.
i was holding her
and i pulled her closer to me
and looked at him like he was fucking nuts.
i held her and hoped
those words didn't even reach her ears.
and even though she was sleeping
i just told her she was okay-
mommy was there.

∽∾

smell

the smell of your baby's hair,
  of a lover's t-shirt-
  of trees after rain,
  of your grandmother's basement-
  of the wharf in san francisco,
  under the sheets after sex-
  of take-out pizza-
  of your father's cologne,
  of turkey in fall,
  of the bakery on wall avenue,
  of blossoms in your mother's yard,
  of heat off of fresh tar,
  of sun tan lotion by the pool-
  of manure on highway 56-
  of snow stinging your nose-
  of your grandfather's minty breath-
  of pine at christmas,
  the smell of everything good
  in everyone's life
everywhere.

celebrate

we celebrated new years
by watching dick clark on t.v.
and right before midnight
i gave him a blow job on the couch.
he said
what did i do to deserve that?
looking back i can honestly say,
not a god damned thing.

making a pearl

there is no getting sand
out of your cunt
after fucking
on a blanket
at the beach.
now there's something
your stupid
fucking romance novels
don't tell you.

๛๛

master

he was soft-spoken
and pretty dorky
but harmless.
my loud mouth seemed to intimidate
the shit out of him.
then he showed me his photo album
of his last girlfriend.
he'd photographed her
in all these bondage poses.
she had the works:
the black vinyl
the dog collar
kneeling before him
and looking up at him
adoringly
while he stuck her
in a cage.
i thought about why he was into
that shit
and i think it had something to do
with why he could never look me in the eye
and why he seemed so afraid
all of the time.

magic

children in swim suits
running outside
in front of a cinderblock house.
the lawn was patchy with burnt gold
sun-stroked grass.
the sprinkler was on
going back and forth
back and forth
and the movement was magical
the water was magical
they ran
and squealed and screamed
capturing the last of summer
from water droplets in their hair.

৽৶

illusions

she told the world a story
but when reality caught up
she changed it.
then she expected us all
to forget.
some of us didn't.

class four

we ate the mushrooms
by the side of the snake river
it was close to midnight
and the shrooms
tasted like dried cow chips.
there was a bunch of us
ready to go down
some class four rapids
in rafts
but me and christy decided on
the inflatable canoe.
we paddled through the calm water
but we could hear
the roar of the first rapids coming up
and the moon was full
so i could see the froth
glowing
and angry ahead
and there was no way for us to paddle away
so i just started pushing through
and screaming
and when we cleared it i couldn't really
stop screaming.
we got through the next stretch
and then
took out near the vans
and christy and justine
tried to calm me down
so they held me by the shoulders
and said
let it go
just let it go.

cracks

my mom accompanied me
on the piano
and i would sing.
back then i sang church songs
but my dad had his fair share
of sinatra and other
big band music
that i got to know, too.
my brother sat in the room next to
the piano room and studied
while i would sing.
eventually i would
go off-key, or
my voice would crack.
my mom would stop playing
so we could start again, but before
she could,
ever so quietly,
my brother would knock on the wall
just to let me know
he'd heard me fuck up.

red betty

i call my convertible
red betty
and she's got some power
behind her.
i take her out
when the day's not stormy
and i take her out
when it's not too hot.
i take her out
when everything's just
perfect.

catch and release

i was with a friend at the bar
and we went home with
these two guys.
my guy was a marine.
someone at the bar said
he'd be a good catch
and so for one night
i caught him.
i think his name was ray.
that morning i got dressed
while he slept
and snuck out
and i left my friend there
with ray's roommate
because she was a big girl
and if you fuck someone like that
you should always have
an exit strategy.
mine was that i drove.

ॐ

choices

he had a knack
for computers
but a love for music-
an innate talent
and gift for music.
the computers paid the bills
while the yearning
in his heart
paid the price.

little mamacita

she was his third
and she was nineteen.
he goes all the way down to mexico
for his little
mamacitas-
they are younger than his daughter.
but it's not like that-
he marries them
because he saves them
and they adore him
and they adore america
and he gets to be
savior
husband
lover
teacher
and all of those things
his bitch ex-wife never saw in him.
they look adoringly at him
with their soft brown eyes
and this one
she has dimples
and an ass like an apple
and they make so much noise for him
when he mounts them,
lumbering his large frame
over their
caramel flesh-
and then something happens to them
when they turn twenty-six
or twenty-seven
and then they all
start to treat him
like his bitch ex-wife.
he thinks he should go
to colombia
next time-
farther south
where they
will never turn their faces away
from him.
he will be enormous
and they will love him
until he's an old man.

inside

there's this woman i know
who is now in her 60s
and she's never had an orgasm.
she's one of those women
who can do everything:
cook, paint, sew
but she can't come.
i think she's so creative
because she's trying to create heaven
outside of herself
when it's been inside her all along.

ৎৡৡ

conference

mr. hyland
picked up
my desk and threw it
into the corner.
the teachers all told
my parents the same thing:
she talks too much.
that,
and
she isn't working up
to her potential.

hustler

in the hustler club
all the waitresses wore corsets.
the girls on stage
danced with
g-strings and tops
and then the second half came
and their tops came off.
i slipped them twenties
then he took them
and he slipped them twenties
and they crawled to him
on hands and knees.

ς∙ℓ

hands

when i go to the gym
i use this one out of the way
bathroom
because i like to pee one more time
before i run.
sometimes someone's in it.
usually it's a guy.
i hear the toilet flush
and then immediately the door opens
like the sink
soap
and paper towels
don't apply to him.
he smiles at me
like he wasn't just wiping his ass
calling it good.

guilty

suicide hotlines
don't tell you anything
you already don't know.
except in my case.
they told me
he had raped me
even though
i was guilty
of letting him in the house.

∽∾

free

fat-free
sugar-free
cholesterol-free
preservative-free
saturated-fat-free
dairy-free
gluten-free
trans-fat-free
organic-free-range
mother-fucking
garbage.

can't

he wasn't even that religious.
we parked up in his fiat
by a church that over-looked
the valley.
we made out
and the windows fogged
making the lights blur
across the windshield
like a colorful constellation.
i was wearing a silky
camisole over my bra
and he had his hand under it.
i pulled the camisole and bra down
and pulled his head toward
my tits.
he said
i can't
like he was some fucking virgin
and i was trying to
shove my cock in.

∽∾

fix

i knew this guy
a friend of a friend
who was supposed to be
a sex addict.
it turned me on a little.
everybody wants to be
somebody's drug
at least for a night.

first pick

my first husband used to
dig for gold
and then force-feed his boogers
to the dog.
yeah
i know.
i picked a real
winner.

❧

escape

nothing out of the ordinary
had happened.
we may have had an ugly fight
the night before.
i stood in the hallway
where the telephone was
and i looked out of the window
and knew
knew
i would leave him.
from that moment
it took two years
and another baby
to plan my escape.

call me crazy

he was from georgia
and had this southern drawl
and we only met once
at a baseball game.
one night he called from atlanta
and it devolved into phone sex.
my first thought was
i could have a bright future in
the business.
my second thought was that
it was the stupidest fucking thing
i've ever done.
pretty soon he called every night
to get off.
he wanted to fly me to san francisco
i suppose to get the real thing.
i agreed at first
but then
the nightly phone calls got to be too much.
i figured out
that nothing i did in person
could possibly match up
to the imaginings
he had in his bed alone.

bff

nothing bonds women
faster
or deeper
than a common enemy.

confession

i don't understand this
fascination
with shaved pussies.
women have said
it's cleaner
and easier.
i'd always thought
cunts were self-cleaning.
most men seem to relish
the shave
but none of them come out
honestly and say
it's because it looks
like a little girl.

∽∾

cheat

when i was 13
there was this guy who went
to my church
who started flirting with me.
he was 22.
i figured i was mature for my age
and that's why he liked me better
than all of the girls his age.
we used to dry hump in his apartment
on his lunch break from work
while i was out of school
for summer.
he told me
he wanted to marry me.
then i found out
he was fucking around with
an 11 year old girl and
it all changed.
i still didn't see him
as a child molesting fuck,
i just saw him as a cheat.

abuse

the girls were eleven
and twelve
and he was only seven.
they made him
put popsicle sticks
into their vaginas.
he maintains he was
never abused.
he was curious.

❧

famous dave's

while watching a man
eat ribs at a
famous dave's bbq
i was forced to go
to my happy place.

chance

it was a big old victorian mansion.
it had been converted into offices
there on south temple.
we drove there in silence
because we'd just had a fight
and i knew i couldn't say anything else
because i promised to
give it a chance.
the woman in the office tried to scare me.
the responsibility.
the financial burden.
the stress.
i was only twenty.
then she reassured me.
the peace of mind.
the freedom.
the chance to know her
later on.
didn't she know
that the moment the doctor told me
i was pregnant
i was bonded to her?
melded to her destiny
and forged as her protector
for life?
but for the sake of my boyfriend
i gave it a chance.
i remember walking out of there
even more determined
than i had been
walking in.
i was going to be a mother.
fuck it.
bring it on.

breath

i knew this kid when i was young
and we played together
all the time.
i got along better with him
than with the girls my age.
he had really bad asthma
and when we'd run a race
i would always win and he would always
have an attack.
we met up later as adults
and we'd fuck
but after
he'd have asthma attacks.
i guess i should have known
he would never keep up.

best

my friend's ex-husband
stopped me outside
a strip club we both happened to be at.
he told me that my ex-boyfriend told him
i was one of the best fucks he'd ever had.
i wanted to tell him
his wife
was one of the best fucks
i'd ever had.
that would have changed the game
a little.

dr. polygamy

i counted.
one, two, three, four…
seven.
seven in all.
seven young women
all dressed in teal medical scrubs.
hovering over them
like a proud
incestuous father
was their boss
a dentist with white hair
a spring in his step
and pigeon chest
proudly puffed out
as he made sure all of his
long-haired
nubile assistants
had their forks and napkins and drinks.
i'm pretty sure i know what
gets him up in the morning.

❧

boston five

there were five of us
around the camp fire.
i liked charles the best
because he was smart
funny
and had his shit together.
they were from boston.
but i ended up in brendan's tent
because he was the hottest one
and charles was kind of shy.
i couldn't help thinking about charles
alone in his tent
while i was with brendan
and my friend was with the other guy.
i wanted to crawl into charles's tent
after
so i could keep talking to him
for days and days
but it occurred to me
that doing that
would be no consolation
to him.

୨୦ବ

belly

i got my belly button pierced
when i was 26
before every eleven year old wanna-be
got theirs done
with the blasé approval
of their disinterested
mothers.
i went to the bar
and danced
and it was so new
this belly-piercing thing
that this guy felt compelled
to pour a corona down the length
of my torso
and lick it off.
my belly ring didn't like corona
and it was red and swollen
for a week.

❧

leaving

i had my kids
seven days out of the week
and then they were gone
for seven days.
i lived with my parents
and i thought it would be okay
to put them to bed
and then leave
to go to the bar
and drink
play pool
get fucked up.
the pain of the kids being there
was as bad
as the pain when they were gone.
they always left, see.
and that pain was worth
a pitcher of beer
and jaeger shots.
i shouldn't have left them
even though they were asleep.
they shouldn't have had to leave me.

ॐ

wonder

if you opened my parent's window
at our old house
there was a 3-foot wide strip of
roof that went along the bottom
of that window.
my mom used to take out the screen
and climb onto that strip
during
thunder and lightning storms.
she always wanted me to come out with her
because she was so excited
by the drama
of the weather.
i went out with her when i was younger
but as i got older
she went out alone.
i wonder why i lost that feeling
of enchantment
with the thunder and lightning.
i wonder why she never did.

❧

caught

my kid caught me
getting fucked from behind
on my parent's living room floor.
i didn't see her
at the door.
she told my mom.
my mom never said anything to me
but my kid did.
she told me what she saw
and so i lied.
i lied my ass off.
i told her i was hugging
her big stuffed teddy bear.
it made no sense
but lying your ass off never does.

drive-by

we were outside on the restaurant patio
near the railing
when a guy rode by on a bike holding something up in the air.
at first
i thought it was a giant joint
and it smelled like pot, too
so i started clapping
along with some other people.
on his second drive-by
i saw that it was sage
not pot
and i remembered suddenly that
i lived in utah
and what else could it be but sage.
it made me a little sad
i wasn't in seattle.

shopping trip

my dad came home from the store
with a light blue kleenex box
to match my room,
pads and tampons
(because i always needed them)
a jar of carmex,
a favorite candy bar.
he did this all the time
and he was so sweet about it
and then my mom would get mad at him
because she only sent him to the store
to get a can of tomatoes.

broken spell

i met the manager of a bookstore.
he had the round glasses of
an intellectual
and the body of a god
and that was a deadly fucking combination.
one night
i picked him up from work
and we drove to an empty lot
and gave each other hand jobs.
the only thing i had on hand to clean him up
was a cloth diaper
from the back seat of my minivan
where the car seat was.
talk about
cognitive fucking dissonance.

❧

booty call

i had an old boyfriend
who would show up about every 3 to 6 months
for sex.
i still had a thing for him
but inside
i knew he would disappear after
and it was totally okay.
when i think about it
i just got to replay
the part of our relationship
that actually worked
and leave out
all the bullshit.

edible

the test kitchen
for a fast food restaurant.
what's that like?
the new
buffalo sauce and bacon
on top of
fried
caramel colored
sodium
and trans-fat
dripping
grease
golden
pattie nuggets
special sauce
wax cheese
preservatives
and dc/orange#2.
i'll have the number
3 please.
super size it.

࿓

big al

when i was 25
i invested in my first
back massager.
i was home alone
and i was watching some
chick flick that had
come on t.v.
i plugged him in
and proceeded to have
24 orgasms in a row.
i felt so superior
to the male species right then.
i realized i was unstoppable.

fault

his father told him
it was his fault he went to jail.
the boy was only nine
and had wanted a pair of shoes.
his father
never seemed to be out
of jail.

৽৹

closet

i dated this guy named todd
who was japanese and italian.
he was model pretty
and very buff
but he had this lisp that
made him sound completely gay.
i was definitely more into
the fucking than he was.
one day at the pool
i saw him hanging around the group of
gay guys that lived in the condo complex.
they all hung around each other
and got tan and buff.
like todd.
he talked about how cool they were
how fun they were
and some time later
he broke up with me
telling me
he just wasn't attracted to me
anymore.
i'd had guys break up with me
before using that excuse
but this time
i didn't take it personally.

eyes

when i was in my late 20s
i learned how to dance
like a stripper.
i made friends with a former
dancer at a club one night
and my whole
hippie-cum-belly dancer action
apparently inspired her to save
me from myself.
she taught me the roll,
undulating my body from my hips
up to my shoulders in a wave.
she taught me how to grind
and i got to use her leg
after she used mine.
she showed me how to bend my knees
and squat all the way
to the floor,
touch my hand on it
and come back up.
it's all in the eyes
she said.
when you're dancing for
or with someone
you gotta look them
right in the eyes.
that's how you get them
she said.
i did what she said
and we danced
and i looked her right in the eyes
and she looked me
right in the eyes
and she was right.
she got me.

ৡৎ

practice

whenever i play the piano
i think of my mother.
i play simple songs,
nothing complex
not too many chords
or flats
or sharps.
my mom, though
she could play chopin
and haydn
and strauss and
rachmaninoff.
so i sit down and play
and i'm so close to
being able to play the hard stuff-
i just need to sit my ass down every day
and practice.
but it's like that.
i'm so close,
like she feels so close,
but it's
so incredibly far away.

ৎৡ

house

they changed everything.
the carpet was blue, then beige.
they took out the carpet and now
it's hardwood and tile.
they tore out the wall separating the kitchen
from the front living room.
there's molding
and two-toned walls.
but the piano is still there
in the basement.
my mother's piano.
my piano.
it's like a hostage
in a house filled with strangers.
i want to knock on the door
and tell them
that's my fucking piano,
but there's no way to
get it out without
tearing out a wall.
my piano is in my house
with strangers
and two-toned walls
and all i can think about
is how mom played chopin
on it
and how
the new owners
have no idea
of the genius
and love and history
that piano has known
and there's no way to tell them
because it's not my house anymore
and the piano
is silent.

છ૭

break-up redux
(broken)

he called me after a month.
would i like to go to dinner?
at dinner we made small talk
got caught up
and he admitted he had missed me.
had i missed him?
i had.
and then after a while he
looked at me and said
you broke me.
i just stared at him
because he was the one
who had the dirty slate
from which i needed to be wiped.
he was the one
who needed to sort things out,
who had said good-bye.
i shook my head-
unbelievable.
no
i said,
it's you who broke me.
then he stood up and pointed to his fly
and said
no, you really broke me.
wanna see?
the details are unimportant.
but in the parking lot
we exchanged hot
heady kisses,
groped each other's bodies
and he let me feel his broken cock.
we made plans to see each other as soon
as possible
and
i had an evil sense of satisfaction
that i broke him.
but i also felt
on some really deep level
that we were done
breaking each other
for good.

daughters

they are so me
and yet they are not me.
i hear them talk about their men,
all of the fine qualities
and all of the things that drive them
nuts
and i think about their fine qualities
and how they must drive their men nuts.
i've learned which daughter won't listen
to me
and which one pretends to
and i've learned
how i taught them
by piss-poor example
how not to be.
there's also good things.
the way one mothers her child
the way the other
gets angry at injustice like me,
the way they laugh.
mostly i want to acknowledge to them
that i know i fucked up
and no matter how hard they try
they're going to fuck up
too.
but the fucked up moments
are when
they see my humanity
and if they can just
look past those
and see the love
they might get it.

ை

liberty park

my grandpa was born
in the middle of liberty park.
his father lived in an old
pioneer house
smack in the middle of the park,
because he was the caretaker.
the park also has an aviary.
you can always hear ducks
in that park,
especially near the big pond.
years later in 1980
a racist serial killer
shot two black guys
jogging
in that park.
he was the same killer who shot
larry flynt.
i bet the ducks were silent
when
those shots came.

❦

survivor

her daughter killed herself.
but she wrote her poetry
and kept coming to our group
and kept breathing
and kept going
and kept painting.
i look at her
and she seems like
a fucking miracle
because
we see her pain
and she lets us
with no apologies.

❦

epilogue

the work

i have been pregnant
for weeks.
four weeks
to be exact—
the daily vomit of words
the back aches
the heart aches
the soul aches
of a mother in hard labor—
and my other children
felt neglected to be sure-
how could i explain that this child
was different than they are
with different needs and different
capabilities—
a special child
that could only incubate
in a short time
and rip me in two
with each
(breath in and out, in and out)
and i don't love the others any less
nor has my care diminished—
but this thing inside of me was demanding
and unrelenting
and for all of its violence
i love it.
so the last push came
and i didn't even know it was over
and out
until it was over-and-out—
and then i marveled at it—
tiny little beginnings
protruding middles
perfect little endings
lined up in a row
with bright eyes…
and a feeling
of wonder came over me
because i didn't know

i had this thing inside
and now that it's out
all i want to do is hold it near me
keep it safe-
but i can't.
like all children
it must be let loose into the world
with its terrible need to judge
and i can only ready it for the blows
as if the violence was for me.

ℬ

the end

JA Carter-Winward lives and writes in the mountains

of northern Utah.

Other works by the author:

Always Listen to the Ravings of a Mad Woman (under Henneman)

TDTM

Falling Back to Earth

Shorts: A Collection (short stories)

The Rub

Coming Soon: *Grind*

www.ingramcontent.com/pod-product-compliance
Lightning Source LLC
Chambersburg PA
CBHW061145040426
42445CB00013B/1561